The school play

John and Marilyn Talbot
Illustrated by Bridget Dowty

'We are going to put on a school play,' said Mr Belter.
'It's called "Jack and the Beanstalk".'

'Ben can play Jack. Tessa can play his mother.
Tony can play the giant,' said Mr Belter.
'Who can I be?' asked Kevin.
'You can be the cow,' said Mr Belter.

All the children were happy.
All the children but Kevin.
He did not want to be the cow.

Then came the opening night.
The curtains went up.

Jack came in.
His mother wasn't happy.
'We have no food,' she said. 'You must take the cow to the market.'

The next day Jack started out for the market.
On the way he met a man.
'I will give you five beans for your cow,' said the man.
'Yes,' said Jack, 'take her.'

But the cow would not go.
'Come on,' said the man.
'No,' said the cow.
'I don't want to go to the market!'

Mr Belter was very surprised.
'Kevin shouldn't say that,' he said.
'I don't want to go to the market,' said Kevin again.
'I don't want to be a cow!'
All the people watching thought it was a joke.
They smiled at one another.

Someone pushed the cow off.
The curtains came down.

The curtains went up again.
Jack gave the beans to his mother.
'Jack, you are a stupid boy,' she said.
She dropped the beans out of the window.

The next day, Jack looked out of the window.
He was surprised.
The beans were a beanstalk now.
It reached up higher than Jack could see.
Jack wanted to go up the beanstalk.

When he reached the top, he saw a white bird lay a gold egg.

But Jack didn't see the giant.
All the children watching the play did.
'He's behind you!' they shouted.
Jack was frightened.

He grabbed the bird and ran.
The giant followed!

Jack came down the beanstalk.
He shouted to his mother, 'The giant is coming!'

Jack gave his mother the bird and the gold egg.
'What a lovely surprise!' she said.

Then Jack hit the beanstalk.
Blow by blow, the beanstalk began to fall.
The giant did too.
That was the end of him!

Jack and his mother were not poor now.
'Jack, you are a clever boy,' said his mother.

The curtains came down.
All the people thought that the school play was good.

Mr Belter was cross with Kevin.
He was going over to tell him off, when
Mr Keeping came over with Mrs Valentine.

'The play was very good,' said Mr Keeping.
'Yes,' said Mrs Valentine, 'the cow was very clever.'
'Clever?' said Mr Belter. He was surprised.
'Yes,' said Mrs Valentine, 'the cow was my favourite!'

Later Mr Belter talked to the children.
'The play was a hit!' he said.

Mr Belter came over to Kevin.
The children watched.
Would Mr Belter tell Kevin off?
'Kevin, your cow was…very clever,'
said Mr Belter.